HIGH-OCTANE CAREERS

AEROSPACE ENGINEER

BY THEIA LAKE

HOT TOPICS

Gareth Stevens PUBLISHING

Please visit our website, www.garethstevens.com. For a free color catalog of all our high-quality books, call toll free 1-800-542-2595 or fax 1-877-542-2596.

Cataloging-in-Publication Data

Names: Lake, Theia.
Title: Aerospace engineer / Theia Lake.
Description: Buffalo, NY : Gareth Stevens Publishing, 2025. | Series: High-octane careers | Includes glossary.
Identifiers: ISBN 9781482469172 (pbk.) | ISBN 9781482469189 (library bound) | ISBN 9781482469196 (ebook)
Subjects: LCSH: Aerospace engineering–Juvenile literature. | Aerospace engineers–Juvenile literature.
Classification: LCC TL793.L25 2025 | DDC 629.1092–dc23

CONTENTS

UP, UP, AND AWAY!

Look to the skies! Picture yourself flying at the speed of sound. What kind of craft would you need to reach great speeds and heights? Could you build it? You could if you were an aerospace engineer! Aerospace engineers use science and math to build aircraft and spacecraft.

UNDER PRESSURE!

The operation, or use, of aircraft is called aviation. Aerospace engineers find ways to make aviation better. They also build spacecraft to search space.

TO THE SKIES AND BEYOND!

There are two fields of aerospace engineering: aeronautical and astronautical. Aeronautics deals with aircraft that fly within Earth's atmosphere. Earth's atmosphere is the mixture of gases that surround the planet. Astronautics deals with spacecraft that fly beyond Earth's atmosphere.

UNDER PRESSURE!

Aerospace engineering, especially astronautics, is sometimes nicknamed "rocket science."

FROM MIND TO MACHINE

Aerospace engineering can be broken into steps:

- Design: planning how to build or improve an aircraft or spacecraft.
- Development: making a prototype.
- Testing: trying out the prototype to find and fix problems.
- Production: overseeing how an aircraft or spacecraft is made.

UNDER PRESSURE!

A prototype is a first model, or form, of something. Aircraft and spacecraft are first designed on computers. Later, they're built as machine prototypes.

SCIENCE IN ACTION

There are a lot of things to think about when building an aircraft or spacecraft. Aerospace engineers need to understand aerodynamics (how things move through the air), physics (the science of matter and energy), and propulsion (how something is pushed forward).

UNDER PRESSURE!

Technology means using science and engineering to come up with useful tools and ways to solve problems. It's also a machine, tool, or way of doing things created by technology.

AIRCRAFT

What kinds of aircraft do aerospace engineers make?

- airplanes
- drones (aircraft without pilots)
- helicopters (aircraft with metal blades that spin around the top)
- jets

Some aircraft are made for many people to use. Others are designed for the military, or armed forces.

HELICOPTER

JET

DRONE

UNDER PRESSURE!

A pilot is someone who flies an aircraft. The development of unmanned aircraft, or aircraft without pilots, is a growing part of the aerospace engineering field.

SPACECRAFT

Spacecraft are made for different purposes and missions, or jobs.

- Rockets carry spacecraft from Earth into space.
- Satellites circle Earth to gather and send information.
- Probes are unmanned spacecraft made to gather facts about places crewed spacecraft can't reach.

PROBE

ROCKET

SATELLITE

UNDER PRESSURE!

Crewed, or manned, spacecraft carry astronauts into space. Seven astronauts live and work on the International Space Station, a spacecraft that orbits, or circles, Earth.

PATH TO THE SKIES

Does the idea of designing aircraft and spacecraft excite you? If so, aerospace engineering might be the job for you! The path to becoming an aerospace engineer isn't easy, but it's well worth the work. Aerospace engineers usually make around $130,000 a year!

UNDER PRESSURE!

Aerospace engineering is a fast-growing field. Jobs for aerospace engineers look to be growing by 6 percent from 2022 to 2032.

AN ENGINEER'S EDUCATION

Young people who hope to become aerospace engineers should study physics and math in high school. Most aerospace engineers need at least a bachelor's, or four-year, **degree** from a college or university. A master's degree can sometimes be completed in five years.

UNDER PRESSURE!

Aerospace engineering is a very competitive field, meaning there are many people trying for jobs. Having a higher level of education can help someone land a job.

HANDS-ON EXPERIENCE

An internship is a temporary, or short-term, work **experience**. In an internship, a student or beginner can learn about an **industry** from a professional, or someone who does a certain job for a living. Internships help engineers gain knowledge and build connections in their field.

UNDER PRESSURE!

Some aerospace engineers choose to get a state **license**. In most states, engineers must have a bachelor's degree, a certain number of years of experience, and pass tests to become licensed.

SOFT SKILLS

In addition to the math and science knowledge that aerospace engineers need, they also need other special skills. Aerospace engineers often work in teams. They need to work well with others and **communicate** clearly. They need to be good problem solvers.

UNDER PRESSURE!

Aerospace engineers must understand the regulations, or rules, about building aircraft and spacecraft. They must also be able to meet deadlines and work within budgets, or certain given amounts of money.

WHERE TO WORK

Aerospace engineers work in different sectors, or areas, such as defense (military), space exploration, and **commercial** aviation. NASA, Boeing, Northrop Grumman, SpaceX, Lockheed Martin, JPL (Jet Propulsion Laboratory), and General Electric are some of the places that hire a lot of aerospace engineers.

UNDER PRESSURE!

Aerospace engineers that work on projects for the military need to pass security, or safety, tests to make sure they're trustworthy and won't share information with outsiders.

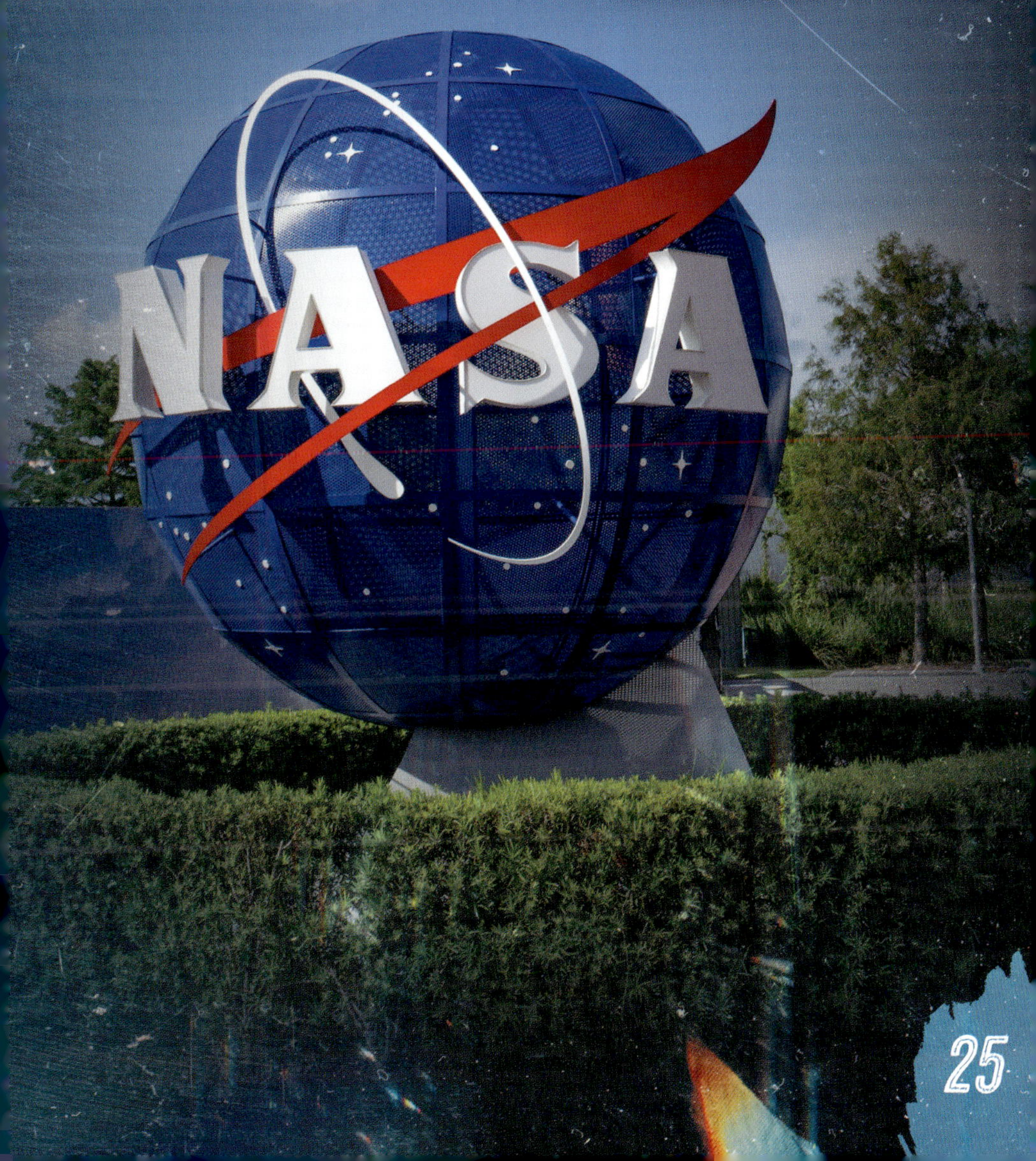

INNOVATORS AND CREATORS

Aerospace engineers are innovators. They come up with new ideas to make aircraft and spacecraft travel go faster and farther, and be better than ever before. These innovations deepen our understanding of Earth, matter, physics, and space. Aerospace technology is truly changing life on Earth.

UNDER PRESSURE!

Spacecraft such as satellites help scientists observe **climate change.** NASA is also developing green technologies, which are meant to be less harmful to the environment.

JASON-3 SATELLITE
studying Earth's oceans and climate change since 1992

GET STARTED!

If aerospace engineering excites you, get started today! Design your own aircraft or build a model rocket! Grow your science and math skills in school. Visit a science museum or check out library books about aviation and space exploration. For an aerospace engineer, even the sky's not the limit!

UNDER PRESSURE!

Experiment with aerodynamics by flying a kite, drone, or paper airplane. Try different ways of making objects fly. An aerospace engineer's greatest tool is their own creativity.

AEROSPACE HEROES

SIR GEORGE CAYLEY (1773-1857)

called the "Father of Aeronautics;" created the idea of a fixed-wing aircraft

ORVILLE WRIGHT (1871-1948) AND WILBUR WRIGHT (1867-1912)

created the first pilot-controlled airplane

WERNHER VON BRAUN (1912-1977)

a leader in the development of rocket technology and space science

DR. KATHERINE JOHNSON (1918-2020)

calculated the trajectory (flight paths) of many important spacecraft missions

KALPANA CHAWLA (1962-2003)

the first Indian woman to go to space

FOR MORE INFORMATION

BOOKS

Finan, Catherine C. *Space Jobs.* Minneapolis, MN: Bearport Publishing, 2022.

Owings, Lisa. *Aerospace Engineer.* Minneapolis, MN: Bellwether Media, 2024.

WEBSITES

NASA
spaceplace.nasa.gov/build-a-spacecraft/en/
Build your own spacecraft on NASA's site for kids!

Science Buddies
www.sciencebuddies.org/blog/aerodynamics-science-projects
Try out fun aerodynamics projects!

Publisher's note to educators and parents: Our editors have carefully reviewed these websites to ensure that they are suitable for students. Many websites change frequently, however, and we cannot guarantee that a site's future contents will continue to meet our high standards of quality and educational value. Be advised that students should be closely supervised whenever they access the internet.

GLOSSARY

climate change: Long-term change in Earth's climate, caused mainly by human activities such as burning oil and natural gas.

commercial: Having to do with commerce, or the buying and selling of things on a large scale.

communicate: To share thoughts or feelings by sound, movement, or writing.

degree: An official paper given to someone who has completed certain classes at a college or university.

experience: Skills gained by doing something.

industry: A group of businesses that provide a certain product or service.

license: A piece of paper that allows someone to do something.

INDEX